# french classics

**THE AUSTRALIAN**
**Women's Weekly**

# contents

The food of France is an art form and is known for its sophistication, but don't let this intimidate you. These recipes are not fussy, they are simple and easy to follow. Try one or two dishes tonight, or create an entirely French feast for family and friends.

*Pamela Clark*

Editorial & Food Director

**Australian cup and spoon measurements are metric. A conversion chart appears on page 77.**

# hors d'oeuvres
# & entrées

Simple and flavoursome, these dishes are a fabulous
way to begin lunch or dinner. Try making two or three
of the hors d'oeuvres for an impressive share-plate.

# pork rillettes with witlof & cornichons

- 1kg (2 pounds) boned pork belly, rind removed, cut into chunks
- 3 bay leaves
- 2 cloves garlic, chopped coarsely
- ¼ cup (60ml) dry white wine
- ¼ cup (60ml) water
- 2 teaspoons salt
- 1 teaspoon ground black pepper
- 1 small red onion (100g), chopped finely
- 1 tablespoon finely chopped fresh flat-leaf parsley
- 6 witlof (belgian endive) (750g), trimmed, leaves separated
- ⅔ cup (120g) drained cornichons

1 Preheat oven to 150°C/300°F.

2 Combine pork, bay leaves, garlic, wine, the water, salt and pepper in a large shallow baking dish.

3 Roast pork mixture, covered, about 2½ hours or until pork is very tender.

4 Discard bay leaves from pork; using two forks, shred pork finely in dish with pan juices. Stir in onion and parsley.

5 Serve pork mixture with witlof and cornichons.

**serving suggestion**
Serve with crusty bread.

**prep + cook time**
3 hours **serves** 8
**nutritional count per serving** 28.1g total fat (9.5g saturated fat); 1551kJ (371 cal); 3.1g carbohydrate; 24.5g protein; 2.8g fibre

# chicken liver pâté

- 1kg (2 pounds) chicken livers
- 200g (6½ ounces) ghee (clarified butter)
- 4 rindless bacon slices (260g)
- 1 small brown onion (80g), chopped finely
- ¼ cup (60ml) brandy
- ½ cup (125ml) pouring cream
- 2 teaspoons finely chopped fresh thyme
- pinch ground nutmeg

**prep + cook time**
45 minutes (+ refrigeration)
**makes** 4 cups
**nutritional count per teaspoon** 1.7g total fat (1g saturated fat); 88kJ (21 cal); 0.1g carbohydrate; 1.2g protein; 0g fibre

1 Cut any sinew from livers; pull each lobe away from connecting tissue.
2 Heat a quarter of the ghee in a large frying pan; cook half the livers, stirring, until browned and barely cooked. Remove from pan. Repeat with another quarter of the ghee and remaining livers.
3 Heat 1 tablespoon of the remaining ghee in same pan; cook bacon and onion, stirring, until onion softens. Add brandy; bring to the boil.

4 Blend livers, bacon mixture, cream, thyme, nutmeg and 2 tablespoons of the remaining ghee until smooth (you may need to do this in batches).
5 Press pâté into a 1-litre (4-cup) dish; melt remaining ghee, pour over pâté in dish. Refrigerate 3 hours or overnight.
**serving suggestion**
Serve with lavosh crispbread, melba toasts or water crackers.

# french onion soup with gruyère croûtons

- 50g (1½ ounces) butter
- 4 large brown onions (800g), sliced thinly
- ¾ cup (180ml) dry white wine
- 3 cups (750ml) water
- 1 litre (4 cups) beef stock
- 1 bay leaf
- 1 tablespoon plain (all-purpose) flour
- 1 teaspoon fresh thyme leaves

### gruyère croûtons
- 1 small french bread stick (150g)
- ½ cup (60g) coarsely grated gruyère cheese

1 Melt butter in a large saucepan; cook onion, stirring occasionally, about 30 minutes or until caramelised.

2 Meanwhile, bring wine to the boil in a large saucepan; boil 1 minute then stir in the water, stock and bay leaf, return to the boil. Remove from heat.

3 Stir flour into onion mixture; cook, stirring, 2 minutes. Gradually add hot broth mixture to onion mixture, stirring, until mixture boils and thickens slightly. Reduce heat; simmer, uncovered, stirring occasionally, 20 minutes. Discard bay leaf; stir in thyme.

4 Meanwhile, make gruyère croûtons.

5 Serve bowls of soup topped with croûtons and some extra thyme leaves, if you like.

### gruyère croûtons
Preheat grill (broiler). Cut bread into 1.5cm (¾-inch) slices. Toast bread under grill on one side then turn and sprinkle with cheese; grill croûtons until cheese browns lightly.

**prep + cook time** 1 hour 15 minutes **serves** 4 **nutritional count per serving** 16.7g total fat (10g saturated fat); 1522kJ (364 cal); 31.1g carbohydrate; 13.4g protein; 3.9g fibre

**tip** A tablespoon of cognac or brandy, stirred into the soup at the last minute, does wonders.

- 320g (10 ounces) sliced smoked salmon
- 1 small red onion (100g), chopped finely
- ½ cup (90g) drained baby capers, rinsed
- 2 small witlof (belgian endive) (110g), leaves separated
- 2 red radishes (70g), trimmed, sliced thinly
- 1 baby fennel bulb (130g), sliced thinly

mustard honey dressing
- 1 teaspoon dijon mustard
- 2 teaspoons honey

- 2 tablespoons lemon juice
- 1 tablespoon finely chopped fresh dill
- ¼ cup (60ml) olive oil

1 Make mustard honey dressing.
2 Divide salmon among serving plates; sprinkle with onion and capers.
3 Serve salmon with witlof, radish and fennel; drizzle with dressing.
**mustard honey dressing** Place ingredients in a screw-top jar; shake well.

# smoked salmon with capers

**prep time** 25 minutes
**serves** 8
**nutritional count per serving** 8.8g total fat (1.3g saturated fat); 564kJ (135 cal); 3.7g carbohydrate; 9.8g protein; 1g fibre

**prep + cook time**
35 minutes **serves** 4
**nutritional count per
serving** 44g total fat
(26.9g saturated fat);
1797kJ (430 cal);
2.8g carbohydrate;
6.1g protein; 2.6g fibre

# asparagus hollandaise

- **1kg (2 pounds) asparagus, trimmed**

**hollandaise sauce**
- **2 tablespoons water**
- **2 tablespoons white wine vinegar**
- **¼ teaspoon cracked black pepper**
- **2 egg yolks**
- **200g (6½ ounces) unsalted butter, melted**

**1** Make hollandaise sauce.
**2** Boil, steam or microwave asparagus until tender.
**3** Serve asparagus on a large platter drizzled with sauce.

**hollandaise sauce** Bring the water, vinegar and pepper to the boil in a small saucepan. Reduce heat; simmer, uncovered, until liquid is reduced to 1 tablespoon. Strain mixture through a fine sieve into a medium heatproof bowl; cool 10 minutes. Whisk egg yolks into vinegar mixture. Set bowl over a medium saucepan of simmering water; do not allow water to touch the base of bowl. Whisk mixture over heat until thickened. Remove bowl from heat; gradually whisk in melted butter in a thin, steady stream, whisking constantly until sauce is thick and creamy.

# goat's cheese soufflé

- 60g (2 ounces) butter
- 1¼ cups (310ml) milk
- 1 teaspoon fresh thyme leaves
- 1 dried bay leaf
- ¼ cup (35g) plain (all-purpose) flour
- 2 egg yolks
- 4 egg whites
- 150g (4½ ounces) mild goat's cheese, crumbled
- ½ cup (125ml) pouring cream
- ⅓ cup (40g) finely grated gruyère cheese

**prep + cook time** 2 hours (+ cooling) **serves** 6
**nutritional count per serving** 27.6g total fat (16.7g saturated fat); 1318kJ (315 cal); 7.5g carbohydrate; 10.1g protein; 0.3g fibre

1 Grease six ⅔-cup (160ml) soufflé dishes using 20g (¾ ounce) of the butter; line each base with baking paper. Place dishes in a large baking dish.
2 Heat milk, thyme and bay leaf in a small saucepan until simmering. Strain into a medium heatproof jug; discard solids. Melt remaining butter in same pan, add flour; cook, stirring, until mixture bubbles and thickens. Gradually stir in hot milk; cook, stirring, until sauce boils and thickens. Transfer to a large heatproof bowl; stir in egg yolks. Cover surface of sauce with plastic wrap; cool.
3 Preheat oven to 180°C/350°F.

4 Beat egg whites in a small bowl with an electric mixer until soft peaks form. Fold a quarter of the egg white into sauce. Fold goat's cheese into sauce, then remaining egg white. Spoon mixture into dishes. Add enough boiling water to baking dish to come half-way up sides of soufflé dishes.
5 Bake soufflés about 15 minutes or until well-puffed. Cool 30 minutes.
6 Unmould soufflés into small ovenproof dishes; place dishes on an oven tray. Spoon a tablespoon of cream over each soufflé; sprinkle with gruyère cheese. Bake soufflés about 10 minutes or until browned lightly.
**serving suggestion** Serve with roasted beetroot (beets).

**tip** Soufflé must be
made just before serving.

# scallops with saffron cream

- 12 scallops in half shell (480g)
- 1 teaspoon olive oil
- 1 small brown onion (80g), chopped finely
- 2 teaspoons finely grated lemon rind
- pinch saffron threads
- ⅔ cup (160ml) pouring cream
- 1 tablespoon lemon juice
- 2 teaspoons salmon roe

1 Remove scallops from shells; wash and dry shells. Place shells, in single layer, on a serving platter.
2 Rinse scallops under cold water; discard scallop roe. Gently pat scallops dry with absorbent paper.
3 Heat oil in a small saucepan; cook onion, stirring, until softened. Add rind, saffron and cream; bring to the boil. Reduce heat; simmer, uncovered, about 5 minutes or until mixture has reduced to about ½ cup. Cool 30 minutes. Stir in juice; stand 10 minutes. Strain cream mixture into a small bowl then back into same cleaned pan; stir over low heat until heated through.

4 Meanwhile, cook scallops, in batches, on heated oiled grill plate (or grill or barbecue) until browned and cooked as desired.
5 Return scallops to shells; top with cream sauce and roe.

**prep + cook time** 15 minutes (+ cooling) **makes** 12 **nutritional count per scallop** 6.4g total fat (4g saturated fat); 288kJ (69 cal); 0.8g carbohydrate; 2.3g protein; 0.1g fibre

# mains

Here you'll find duck confit with pear & watercress salad, coq au vin and boeuf bourguignon to name just a few. Delicious, classic recipes that no cook should be without.

# pork chops with apples & calvados

- 4 x 280g (9½-ounce) pork loin chops
- 45g (1½ ounces) butter
- 2 medium apples (300g), peeled, cut into thin wedges
- 4 shallots (100g), sliced thinly
- 1 tablespoon plain (all-purpose) flour
- ½ cup (125ml) calvados
- 1 cup (250ml) cider vinegar
- 1 cup (250ml) chicken stock
- ⅔ cup (160ml) pouring cream

1 Cook pork in a heated oiled large frying pan. Remove from pan; cover to keep warm. Drain and discard excess fat from pan.

2 Heat half the butter in pan; cook apples, stirring, until browned lightly. Remove from pan.

3 Heat remaining butter in pan; cook shallots, stirring, until soft. Add flour; cook, stirring, 1 minute. Add calvados; bring to the boil. Stir in vinegar, stock and cream; simmer, uncovered, until sauce thickens slightly. Return apples to pan; cook until heated through.

4 Serve pork topped with apples and sauce.

**serving suggestion**
Serve with a green salad.

**prep + cook time** 30 minutes **serves** 4
**nutritional count per serving** 47.5g total fat (25g saturated fat); 2947kJ (705 cal); 18.1g carbohydrate; 35.7g protein; 1.4g fibre

**tip** Calvados is an apple-flavoured brandy made in Normandy; regular brandy can be used instead.

**tip** Persillade is a mixture of chopped garlic and parsley, traditionally used either as a garnish or to flavour a sauce, as we have done here.

# seared calves' liver with persillade

- 400g (12½-ounce) piece calves' liver, sliced thinly
- 50g (1½ ounces) butter
- 1 clove garlic, chopped finely
- 1 shallot (25g), chopped finely
- ½ cup (125ml) chicken stock
- 1 tablespoon lemon juice
- ⅓ cup finely chopped fresh flat-leaf parsley

1 Pat liver dry with absorbent paper. Melt 1 tablespoon of the butter in a large frying pan; cook liver quickly, in batches, over high heat until browned both sides and cooked as desired (do not overcook). Remove from pan; cover to keep warm.

2 To make persillade, heat remaining butter in same pan; cook garlic and shallot, stirring, until shallot softens. Add stock and juice; bring to the boil, stirring. Remove from heat; stir in parsley.

3 Serve sliced liver topped with persillade.

serving suggestion Serve with creamy mashed potato and steamed asparagus.

prep + cook time 30 minutes serves 4 nutritional count per serving 18g total fat (9.1g saturated fat); 1087kJ (260 cal); 3g carbohydrate; 21.6g protein; 0.3g fibre

# quiche lorraine

- 1 medium brown onion (150g), chopped finely
- 3 rindless bacon slices (195g), chopped finely
- 3 eggs
- 300ml (½ pint) pouring cream
- ½ cup (125ml) milk
- ¾ cup (120g) coarsely grated gruyère cheese

## pastry

- 1¾ cups (260g) plain (all-purpose) flour
- 155g (5 ounces) cold butter, chopped coarsely
- 1 egg yolk
- 2 teaspoons lemon juice
- ⅓ cup (80ml) iced water, approximately

**1** Make pastry.

**2** Preheat oven to 200°C/400°F.

**3** Roll pastry between sheets of baking paper until large enough to line a deep 23cm loose-based flan tin. Lift pastry into tin; gently press pastry around side. Trim edge, place tin on oven tray. Cover pastry with baking paper; fill with dried beans or rice. Bake 10 minutes; remove paper and beans. Bake pastry a further 10 minutes or until golden brown; cool.

**4** Reduce oven temperature to 180°C/350°F.

**5** Cook onion and bacon in a heated oiled small frying pan until onion is soft; drain on absorbent paper, cool. Sprinkle bacon mixture over pastry case.

**6** Whisk eggs in a medium bowl then whisk in cream, milk and cheese; pour into pastry case. Bake, in the oven, about 35 minutes or until filling is set. Stand 5 minutes before removing quiche from tin.

**pastry** Sift flour into bowl; rub in butter. Add egg yolk, juice and enough of the water to make ingredients cling together. Knead gently on a lightly floured surface until smooth; cover, refrigerate 30 minutes.

**prep + cook time** 1 hour 30 minutes (+ refrigeration) **serves** 6 **nutritional count per serving** 51.8g total fat (35.4g saturated fat); 3139kJ (751 cal); 35.4g carbohydrate; 22.1g protein; 2g fibre

**prep + cook time** 2 hours 30 minutes **serves** 6 **nutritional count per serving** 8.6g total fat (2.7g saturated fat); 1714kJ (410 cal); 20g carbohydrate; 57.2g protein; 11.7g fibre

# pot au feu with cabbage rolls

- 2 veal shanks (1.5kg)
- 2 large carrots (360g), chopped coarsely
- 1 medium leek (350g), chopped coarsely
- 2 small turnips (300g), chopped coarsely
- 6 baby onions (150g)
- 1 bay leaf
- 3 cups (750ml) chicken stock
- 1 litre (4 cups) water
- 1 small savoy cabbage (1.2kg)
- 250g (8 ounces) minced (ground) pork
- 250g (8 ounces) minced (ground) chicken
- 1 egg
- 1 small brown onion (80g), chopped finely
- ½ cup (50g) packaged breadcrumbs

1 Place veal, carrot, leek, turnip, whole onions, bay leaf, stock and the water in a large saucepan; bring to the boil. Reduce heat; simmer, uncovered, about 1½ hours or until veal is tender. Remove veal; when cool enough to handle, separate meat from bones and chop coarsely.

2 Remove 12 large leaves from cabbage; cook, uncovered, in batches, in a large saucepan of boiling water for 3 minutes. Drain leaves on absorbent paper. Finely chop enough of the remaining cabbage to make ⅓ cup; reserve remaining cabbage for another use.

3 Meanwhile, using hands, combine pork, chicken, egg, onion, breadcrumbs and chopped cabbage in a large bowl; divide mixture between cabbage leaves. Roll leaves to enclose filling, secure with toothpicks.

4 Return veal meat to vegetable mixture in pan, add cabbage rolls; bring to the boil. Reduce heat; simmer, uncovered, about 10 minutes or until cabbage rolls are cooked through.

5 Divide cabbage rolls among serving bowls; ladle soup over the top.

**tips** The literal translation of "pot on the fire" refers to the way this old recipe was originally cooked, in a huge cast-iron pot directly in the fireplace. Any combination of vegetables and meat can be used, and the French versions are as numerous as there are regions of the country. When peeling turnips, make sure you remove all the bitter outer layer.

# fish stew with saffron, tomato & wine

- 500g (1 pound) uncooked medium king prawns (shrimp)
- 500g (1 pound) small mussels
- 1 tablespoon olive oil
- 1 medium brown onion (150g), chopped finely
- 3 cloves garlic, crushed
- 1 small leek (200g), sliced thinly
- 1 small fennel bulb (200g), sliced thinly
- 1 stalk celery (150g), trimmed, sliced thinly
- ½ cup (125ml) dry white wine
- 800g (1½ pounds) canned diced tomatoes
- 1 litre (4 cups) fish stock
- pinch saffron threads
- 200g (6½ ounces) kipfler (fingerling) potatoes, cut into 1cm (½-inch) slices
- 300g (9½ ounces) skinless firm white fish fillet, chopped coarsely
- 300g (9½ ounces) skinless salmon fillet, chopped coarsely

1 Shell and devein prawns. Scrub mussels; remove beards.

2 Heat oil in a large flameproof dish; cook onion, garlic, leek, fennel and celery, stirring, about 10 minutes or until vegetables soften.

3 Add wine, undrained tomatoes, stock, saffron and potato to pan; bring to the boil. Reduce heat; simmer, uncovered, about 10 minutes or until potato is tender.

4 Add prawns and fish to pan; cook, uncovered, 5 minutes. Add mussels; cook, covered, about 2 minutes or until mussels open (discard any that do not).

**prep + cook time** 1 hour **serves** 6 **nutritional count per serving** 9g total fat (1.9g saturated fat); 1254kJ (300 cal); 13.5g carbohydrate; 35.4g protein; 4.3g fibre

**prep + cook time** 4 hours
**serves** 6 **nutritional count
per serving** 184.2g total fat
(41.6g saturated fat); 8628kJ
(2064 cal); 24.5g carbohydrate;
79.9g protein; 5.5g fibre

# duck confit with pear & watercress salad

- 2 x 2kg (4-pound) whole ducks
- 1 tablespoon coarse cooking (kosher) salt
- 2 cloves garlic, sliced thinly
- 1 bay leaf, crumbled
- 2 sprigs fresh thyme
- 2 teaspoons black peppercorns
- 2 cups (500ml) olive oil
- 750g (1½ pounds) kipfler (fingerling) potatoes, halved lengthways

## pear & watercress salad

- 1 tablespoon wholegrain mustard
- 1 tablespoon white wine vinegar
- 1 teaspoon white sugar
- ¼ cup (60ml) olive oil
- 3 cups (350g) firmly packed trimmed watercress
- 1 large pear (330g), sliced thinly

1 Using sharp knife, cut marylands and breasts off ducks. Remove as much fat as possible from carcasses; reserve. Discard wings and carcasses.

2 Combine duck pieces, salt, garlic, bay leaf, thyme and peppercorns in a medium bowl. Cover; refrigerate until required.

3 Meanwhile, place reserved fat in a large saucepan; cook, uncovered, over low heat, about 1 hour or until fat has melted. Strain mixture through a fine sieve into a large bowl; discard solids (you will have about 2 cups of duck fat).

4 Preheat oven to 150°C/300°F.

5 Rinse duck pieces under cold water; pat dry with absorbent paper. Place duck pieces, in a single layer, in a large baking dish. Reserve 2 tablespoons of the fat; pour remaining fat over duck. Top up with olive oil, making sure duck is completely submerged. Roast, uncovered, 2 hours.

6 Boil, steam or microwave potatoes until tender; drain. Heat reserved fat in a large frying pan; cook potato, in batches, until browned. Remove from pan; cover to keep warm.

7 Meanwhile, make pear and watercress salad.

8 Place duck in same large frying pan; cook, skin-side down, until skin is crisp. Serve duck with potato and salad.

pear and watercress salad Place mustard, vinegar, sugar and oil in screw-top jar; shake well. Place watercress, pear and dressing in a large bowl; toss gently to combine.

# coq au vin

- 750g (1½ pounds) spring onions
- ¼ cup (60ml) olive oil
- 6 rindless bacon slices (390g), chopped coarsely
- 310g (10½ ounces) button mushrooms
- 2 cloves garlic, crushed
- 8 chicken thigh fillets (880g)
- ¼ cup (35g) plain (all-purpose) flour
- 2 cups (500ml) dry red wine
- 1½ cups (375ml) chicken stock
- 2 tablespoons tomato paste
- 3 bay leaves
- 4 sprigs fresh thyme
- 2 sprigs fresh rosemary

1 Trim green ends from onions, leaving about 4cm (1½ inches) of stem attached; trim roots. Heat 1 tablespoon of the oil in a large frying pan; cook onions, stirring, until browned; remove from pan.

2 Add bacon, mushrooms and garlic to pan; cook, stirring, until bacon is crisp. Remove from pan.

3 Coat chicken in flour; shake off excess. Heat remaining oil in same pan; cook chicken, in batches, until browned. Drain on absorbent paper.

4 Return chicken to pan with wine, stock, paste, bay leaves, herbs, onions and bacon mixture. Bring to the boil; reduce heat, simmer, uncovered, about 35 minutes or until chicken is tender and sauce has thickened slightly.

**prep + cook time**
1 hour 30 minutes
**serves** 4
**nutritional count per**
**serving** 43.6g total fat
(11.8g saturated fat);
3428kJ (820 cal);
16.3g carbohydrate;
67.8g protein; 6.4g fibre

**prep + cook time** 2 hours 50 minutes (+ standing) **serves** 6  **nutritional count per serving** 28.2g total fat (10.5g saturated fat); 2750kJ (658 cal); 38.5g carbohydrate; 55.8g protein; 12.4g fibre

# cassoulet

- 1½ cups (300g) dried white beans
- 300g (9½ ounces) boned pork belly, rind removed, sliced thinly
- 150g (4½-ounce) piece streaky bacon, rind removed, cut into 1cm (½-inch) pieces
- 800g (1½-pound) piece boned lamb shoulder, cut into 2.5cm (1-inch) pieces
- 1 large brown onion (200g), chopped finely
- 1 small leek (200g), sliced thinly
- 2 cloves garlic, crushed
- 3 sprigs fresh thyme
- 400g (12½ ounces) canned crushed tomatoes
- 2 dried bay leaves
- 1 cup (250ml) water
- 1 cup (250ml) chicken stock
- 2 cups (140g) stale breadcrumbs
- ⅓ cup coarsely chopped fresh flat-leaf parsley

1 Place beans in a medium bowl, cover with cold water. Stand overnight, drain; rinse under cold water, drain. Cook beans in a medium saucepan of boiling water about 15 minutes or until tender; drain.

2 Preheat oven to 160°C/325°F.

3 Cook pork belly in a large flameproof dish, pressing down with back of spoon on pork until browned; remove from dish. Cook bacon in same pan, stirring, until crisp; remove from dish. Cook lamb, in batches, in same pan, until browned. Remove from dish.

4 Cook onion, leek and garlic in same dish, stirring, until onion softens. Return meat to dish with thyme, undrained tomatoes, bay leaves, the water, stock and beans; bring to the boil. Cover; cook, in oven, 45 minutes. Remove from oven; season to taste, sprinkle with combined breadcrumbs and parsley. Cook, uncovered, in oven, about 45 minutes or until liquid is nearly absorbed and beans are tender.

**tip** This is a traditional recipe from the Languedoc region in the south west of France. There are many variations: with duck or goose fat, with or without lamb, tomato, toulouse sausages or duck confit.

# boeuf bourguignon

- 280g (9 ounces) baby brown onions
- 2 tablespoons olive oil
- 2kg (4 pounds) gravy beef, trimmed, chopped
- 30g (1 ounce) butter
- 2 cloves garlic, crushed
- 4 rindless bacon slices (260g), chopped coarsely
- 400g (13 ounces) button mushrooms, halved
- ¼ cup (35g) plain (all-purpose) flour
- 1¼ cups (310ml) beef stock
- 2½ cups (625ml) dry red wine
- 2 bay leaves
- 2 sprigs fresh thyme
- ½ cup coarsely chopped fresh flat-leaf parsley

1 Peel onions, leaving root end intact so onion remains whole during cooking.

2 Heat oil in a large flameproof dish; cook beef, in batches, until browned. Remove from pan.

3 Add butter to dish; cook onions, garlic, bacon and mushrooms, stirring, until onions brown lightly.

4 Sprinkle flour over onion mixture; cook, stirring, until flour mixture thickens and bubbles. Gradually add stock and wine; stir over heat until mixture boils and thickens.

5 Return beef and any juices to dish, add bay leaves and thyme; bring to the boil. Reduce heat; simmer, covered, about 2 hours or until beef is tender, stirring every 30 minutes. Remove from heat; discard bay leaves. Stir in parsley.

**prep + cook time** 2 hours 45 minutes **serves** 6 **nutritional count per serving** 31.4g total fat (12.1g saturated fat); 2658kJ (636 cal); 6.6g carbohydrate; 80.3g protein; 2.8g fibre

**tip** This is a traditional dish from the Burgundy region (*Bourgogne*) known for its beef (charolais) and its wine.

# vegetables
# & salads

French food revolves around choosing the best produce you can find, and then taking the time to savour it. Using garden-fresh vegetables in these dishes will make all the difference.

# dill & caper potato salad

- 1kg (2 pounds) baby potatoes, unpeeled, halved
- 2 tablespoons white wine vinegar
- ½ cup (125ml) olive oil
- ½ teaspoon white sugar
- 1 teaspoon dijon mustard
- ⅓ cup (65g) drained baby capers, rinsed
- ⅔ cup (140g) drained pickled cocktail onions, halved
- 1 cup (200g) drained cornichons, halved lengthways
- 2 tablespoons coarsely chopped fresh dill

1 Boil, steam or microwave potato until just tender; drain.

2 Meanwhile, place vinegar, oil, sugar and mustard in a screw-top jar; shake well.

3 Combine potato and half the dressing in a large bowl; cool 10 minutes.

4 Add capers, onion, cornichons, dill and remaining dressing to salad; toss gently to combine.

**prep + cook time** 30 minutes **serves** 4 **nutritional count per serving** 28.8g total fat (4g saturated fat); 1885kJ (451 cal); 40g carbohydrate; 6.4g protein; 5.1g fibre

**tips** You can buy pickled cocktail onions and cornichons from most supermarkets. You can also use pink fir apple or ruby lou potatoes for this recipe.

**prep + cook time** 1 hour
10 minutes **serves** 6
**nutritional count per
serving** 13.9g total fat
(9g saturated fat); 1066kJ
(255 cal); 26.3g carbohydrate;
4.9g protein; 3.2g fibre

# potatoes anna

- 1.2kg (4 pounds) ruby lou potatoes, peeled
- 100g (3 ounces) butter, melted

1 Preheat oven to 240°C/475°F. Oil a shallow 2-litre (8-cup), 26cm (10½-inch) round baking dish.

2 Using sharp knife, mandoline or V-slicer, slice potatoes into 2mm (⅛-inch) slices; pat dry with absorbent paper. Place a single layer of potato, slightly overlapping, into baking dish; brush with a little of the butter. Continue layering remaining potato and butter.

3 Cover dish with foil; bake 20 minutes. Remove foil; use metal spatula to press down on potato.

4 Reduce oven to 220°C/425°F; bake, uncovered, about 30 minutes or until top is crisp and browned. Cut into wedges to serve.

**tips** In the late 1800s, French chef Adolphe Dugléré devised this dish in honour of Anna Deslions, a courtesan who entertained clients in a private dining room within his restaurant. You can also use coliban potatoes for this recipe.

- 20g (¾ ounces) butter
- 625g (1¼ pounds) spinach, trimmed
- ½ cup (125ml) pouring cream

**1** Melt butter in a large frying pan; cook spinach, stirring, until wilted.

**2** Add cream; bring to the boil. Reduce heat; simmer, uncovered, until liquid reduces by half.

**prep + cook time** 15 minutes **serves** 4 **nutritional count per serving** 38.7g total fat (25.4g saturated fat); 1555kJ (372 cal); 2.8g carbohydrate; 3.5g protein; 2.1g fibre

# creamed spinach

# celeriac puree

- 2 cups (500ml) chicken stock
- 1kg (2 pounds) celeriac (celery root), trimmed, peeled, chopped coarsely
- ½ cup (125ml) pouring cream
- 1 tablespoon finely chopped fresh chives

1 Bring stock to the boil in a medium saucepan; add celeriac, return to the boil. Reduce heat; simmer, covered, about 30 minutes or until celeriac is tender. Drain.
2 Blend or process celeriac in batches with cream until smooth.
3 Serve sprinkled with chives.

**serving suggestion**
Serve with seafood, poultry or game birds such as quail or squab pigeon.

**prep + cook time**
35 minutes **serves** 4
**nutritional count per serving** 14.4g total fat (9.2g saturated fat); 815kJ (195 cal); 7.4g carbohydrate; 5.2g protein; 8.8g fibre

# witlof, pear & roquefort salad

- 2 red witlof (belgian endive) (250g), trimmed, leaves separated
- 2 yellow witlof (belgian endive) (250g), trimmed, leaves separated
- 1 medium pear (230g), sliced thinly
- ¾ cup (90g) roasted pecans, coarsely chopped

### blue cheese dressing
- ⅓ cup (80ml) buttermilk
- 100g (3 ounces) roquefort cheese, crumbled
- 1 tablespoon lemon juice

1 Make blue cheese dressing.
2 Place salad ingredients in a large bowl; toss gently to combine.
3 Serve salad drizzled with dressing.

**blue cheese dressing**
Whisk ingredients in a small jug until smooth.

**prep time** 20 minutes
**serves** 4
**nutritional count per serving** 24.9g total fat (6.5g saturated fat); 1295kJ (309 cal); 9.9g carbohydrate; 9.5g protein; 5.3g fibre

**tips** Witlof is a perfect addition to this bitey salad. Its bitter-yet-creamy flavour goes beautifully with the sharp taste of the blue cheese, and its crisp, robust nature makes it a perfect candidate for the rich dressing. Choose another sharp blue cheese if you cannot find roquefort.

- 3 small potatoes (360g), chopped coarsely
- 200g (6½ ounces) baby green beans, trimmed
- 2 tablespoons olive oil
- 1 tablespoon lemon juice
- 2 tablespoons white wine vinegar
- 4 medium tomatoes (600g), cut into wedges
- 4 hard-boiled eggs, quartered
- 425g (13½ ounces) canned tuna in springwater, drained, flaked
- ½ cup (80g) rinsed, drained caperberries
- ½ cup (60g) seeded small black olives
- ¼ cup firmly packed fresh flat-leaf parsley leaves

1 Boil, steam or microwave potato and beans, separately, until tender; drain. Rinse under cold water; drain.

2 Whisk oil, juice and vinegar in a large bowl; add potatoes, beans and remaining ingredients, toss gently to combine.

**prep + cook time** 20 minutes **serves** 4 **nutritional count per serving** 17g total fat (3.7g saturated fat); 1530kJ (366 cal); 18.9g carbohydrate; 30.9g protein; 4.9g fibre

# salade nicoise

**tip** This is a specialty from Nice in the South of France.

**tip** French-style green lentils are the Australian variety of lentils du puy. They are perfect for salads as they keep their shape after cooking.

# warm lentil & chorizo salad

- 1¼ cups (250g) french-style green lentils
- 1 small brown onion (80g), quartered
- 1 bay leaf
- 2 cured chorizo sausages (340g), sliced thinly
- ½ cup (125ml) red wine vinegar
- ⅓ cup (80ml) olive oil
- 3 shallots (75g), sliced thinly
- 2 stalks celery (300g), trimmed, sliced diagonally
- 1 cup coarsely chopped fresh flat-leaf parsley

1 Cook lentils, onion and bay leaf in a large saucepan of boiling water, uncovered, about 15 minutes or until lentils are tender; drain. Discard onion and bay leaf.

2 Cook chorizo in a large frying pan, stirring occasionally, until browned. Drain; cool 10 minutes.

3 Place vinegar and oil in a screw-top jar; shake well.

4 Place lentils and chorizo in a large bowl with shallot, celery, parsley and dressing; toss gently to combine.

**prep + cook time**
40 minutes **serves** 6
**nutritional count per serving** 30g total fat (8g saturated fat); 1848kJ (442 cal); 18.9g carbohydrate; 28.1g protein; 7.2g fibre

# braised baby leeks

- **16 baby pencil leeks (1.3kg)**
- **30g (1 ounce) butter**
- **⅔ cup (160ml) chicken stock**
- **2 tablespoons dry white wine**
- **1 teaspoon finely grated lemon rind**
- **2 tablespoons lemon juice**
- **¼ cup (20g) shaved parmesan cheese**
- **¼ cup coarsely chopped fresh flat-leaf parsley**

**1** Carefully trim root end from leeks, leaving each leek in one piece. Trim leeks into 15cm (6-inch) lengths; halve lengthways. Rinse under cold water; drain.

**2** Melt butter in a large frying pan; cook leeks, 1 minute. Add stock, wine, rind and juice; bring to the boil. Reduce heat; simmer, covered, 15 minutes or until leeks are tender. Uncover; simmer about 5 minutes or until liquid has reduced by half.

**3** Serve leeks drizzled with cooking liquid, sprinkled with cheese and parsley.

**tip** You could serve these leeks on their own as a first course, or as an impressive side to veal or fish. Be sure to supply diners with sharp knives, as even baby leeks can be a bit difficult to cut.

prep + cook time
40 minutes **serves** 4
**nutritional count per
serving** 8.7g total fat
(5.2g saturated fat);
644kJ (154 cal);
8.3g carbohydrate;
6.5g protein; 6g fibre

# after-dinner treats

French desserts are delicate and decadent all at once. Serve any of these gorgeous sweet things as the elegant finale to a delicious meal. Enjoy with coffee, or french vanilla ice-cream.

# chocolate soufflé

- ⅓ cup (75g) caster (superfine) sugar
- 50g (1½ ounces) butter
- 1 tablespoon plain (all-purpose) flour
- 200g (6½ ounces) dark eating (semi-sweet) chocolate, melted
- 2 eggs, separated
- 2 egg whites
- 1 tablespoon cocoa powder

1 Preheat oven to 180°C/350°F. Grease four ¾-cup (180ml) soufflé dishes. Sprinkle inside of dishes with a little of the sugar; shake away excess. Place dishes on an oven tray.

2 Melt butter in a small saucepan, add flour; cook, stirring, about 2 minutes or until mixture thickens and bubbles. Remove from heat; stir in chocolate and egg yolks. Transfer to a large bowl.

3 Beat all egg whites in a small bowl with an electric mixer until soft peaks form. Gradually add remaining sugar, beating until sugar dissolves. Fold egg white mixture into chocolate mixture, in two batches. Spoon soufflé mixture into dishes.

4 Bake soufflés 15 minutes. Serve immediately, dusted with cocoa powder.

**tips** Egg whites are vital to a soufflé's success. They must be folded very carefully into the mixture. Use a wide-topped bowl so folding is easier for you. Use a whisk, spatula or large metal spoon for the folding. Some cooks like to fold a small amount of the egg white (about a quarter) through the flavoured, more solid mixture first to "let the mixture down" a little. Fold in the remaining egg whites, in one or two batches depending on the quantity. Soufflés must be made just before serving.

**prep + cook time**
35 minutes **serves** 4
**nutritional count per
serving** 27.1g total fat
(16.1g saturated fat);
2040kJ (488 cal);
52.3g carbohydrate;
8.1g protein; 0.7g fibre

# tarte tatin

- **6 large apples (1.2kg)**
- **100g (3 ounces) unsalted butter, chopped**
- **1 cup (220g) firmly packed light brown sugar**
- **2 tablespoons lemon juice**

**pastry**

- **1 cup (150g) plain (all-purpose) flour**
- **2 tablespoons caster (superfine) sugar**
- **80g (2¾ ounces) cold unsalted butter, chopped**
- **2 tablespoons sour cream**

**prep + cook time**
2 hours 30 minutes
(+ refrigeration) **serves** 8
**nutritional count per serving** 21.1g total fat
(13.7g saturated fat);
1860kJ (445 cal);
59.5g carbohydrate;
2.7g protein; 2.9g fibre

1 Peel, core and quarter apples. Melt butter in a large heavy-based frying pan; add apple, sprinkle evenly with sugar and juice. Cook, uncovered, over low heat, for 1 hour, turning apple as it caramelises.

2 Place apple, rounded-side down, in 24cm (9½-inch) pie dish; drizzle with 1 tablespoon of the caramel in pan. Reserve remaining caramel. Pack apples tightly to avoid any gaps. Cover; refrigerate until required.

3 Make pastry.

4 Preheat oven to 200°C/400°F.

5 Roll dough between sheets of baking paper until large enough to cover apple. Peel away one sheet of baking paper; invert pastry over apple. Remove remaining paper; tuck pastry around apple.

6 Bake tarte tartin about 30 minutes or until browned. Carefully turn onto serving plate.

7 Reheat reserved caramel over low heat; drizzle over apples.

**pastry** Process flour, sugar, butter and sour cream until ingredients just come together. Knead dough on floured surface until smooth. Cover; refrigerate 30 minutes.

# palmiers

- **2 tablespoons raw sugar**
- **1 sheet puff pastry**
- **1 teaspoon ground nutmeg**

**prep + cook time**
35 minutes (+ cooling)
**makes** 30 **nutritional count
per palmier** 1.3g total fat
(0.1g saturated fat); 105kJ
(25 cal); 3.1g carbohydrate;
0.3g protein; 0.1g fibre

**1** Preheat oven to 180°C/350°F. Grease two oven trays; line with baking paper.
**2** Sprinkle a board lightly with a little of the sugar. Roll pastry on sugared board into a 20cm x 30cm (8-inch x 12-inch) rectangle; trim edges. Sprinkle pastry with nutmeg and remaining sugar.

**3** Starting from long side, loosely roll one side at a time into the middle of the rectangle, so the two long sides meet in the centre. Cut pastry into 1cm (½-inch) thick slices. Place, cut-side up, about 5cm (2 inches) apart, on trays. Spread pastry open slightly at folded ends to make a V-shape.
**4** Bake palmiers about 15 minutes or until golden brown; transfer to wire rack to cool.

prep + cook time 55 minutes
(+ refrigeration) serves 6
**nutritional count per
serving** 52.1g total fat
(32.3g saturated fat); 2358kJ
(564 cal); 19.8g carbohydrate;
5.8g protein; 8g fibre

# crème brûlée

- 1 vanilla bean
- 3 cups (750ml) thickened (heavy) cream
- 6 egg yolks
- ¼ cup (55g) caster (superfine) sugar
- ¼ cup (40g) pure icing (confectioners') sugar

**tips** Make sure you place the crème brûlées as close as possible to the hot grill. Surrounding the custards with ice keeps them cool as you heat the top. Of course, you could use a blowtorch if you have one. The adjustable flame melts the sugar quickly so the filling remains cool. Professional cooks' blowtorches are available from specialty kitchen shops.

1 Preheat oven to 180°C/350°F. Grease six ½-cup (125ml) ovenproof dishes.

2 Split vanilla bean in half lengthways; scrape seeds into a medium heatproof bowl. Place pod in a small saucepan with cream; heat without boiling.

3 Add egg yolks and caster sugar to seeds in bowl; gradually whisk in hot cream mixture. Place bowl over a medium saucepan of simmering water; stir over heat about 10 minutes or until custard mixture thickens slightly and coats the back of a spoon. Discard vanilla pod.

4 Place small dishes in a large baking dish; spoon custard into dishes. Add enough boiling water to baking dish to come halfway up the sides of small dishes.

5 Bake custards, uncovered, about 20 minutes or until set. Remove custards from dish; cool. Cover; refrigerate overnight.

6 Preheat grill (broiler).

7 Place custards in a shallow flameproof dish filled with ice cubes; sprinkle custards evenly with sifted icing sugar. Using your finger, spread sugar over the surface of each custard, pressing in gently; place under grill until the tops caramelise.

# crème caramel

- ¾ cup (165g) caster (superfine) sugar
- ½ cup (125ml) water
- 6 eggs
- 1 teaspoon vanilla extract
- ½ cup (75g) caster (superfine) sugar, extra
- 300ml (½ pint) pouring cream
- 1¾ cups (430ml) milk

> **prep + cook time** 1 hour (+ refrigeration) **serves** 8
> **nutritional count per serving** 22.3g total fat (13.3g saturated fat); 1526kJ (365 cal); 33.8g carbohydrate; 7.5g protein; 0g fibre

**1** Preheat oven to 160°C/325°F.

**2** Stir sugar and the water in a medium heavy-based frying pan over heat, without boiling, until sugar dissolves. Bring to the boil; boil, uncovered, without stirring, until mixture is a deep caramel colour. Remove from heat; allow bubbles to subside. Pour toffee into a deep 20cm (8-inch) round cake pan.

**3** Whisk eggs, extract and extra sugar in a large bowl.

**4** Bring cream and milk to the boil in a medium saucepan. Whisking constantly, pour hot milk mixture into egg mixture. Strain mixture into cake pan.

**5** Place pan in a baking dish; add enough boiling water to come halfway up side of pan. Bake about 40 minutes or until set.

**6** Remove crème caramel from baking dish. Cover; refrigerate overnight.

**7** Gently ease crème caramel from side of pan; invert onto a deep-sided serving plate.

**tip** To make orange madeleines, add 1 teaspoon finely grated orange rind when beating the egg mixture. Omit the water and replace with 1 tablespoon orange juice.

# madeleines

- 2 eggs
- 2 tablespoons caster (superfine) sugar
- 2 tablespoons icing (confectioners') sugar
- ¼ cup (35g) self-raising flour
- ¼ cup (35g) plain (all-purpose) flour
- 75g (2½ ounces) unsalted butter, melted
- 1 tablespoon water
- 2 tablespoons icing (confectioners') sugar, extra

1 Preheat oven to 200°C/400°F. Grease two 12-hole (1½-tablespoon/30ml) madeleine pans.
2 Beat eggs and sifted sugars in a small bowl with an electric mixer until thick and creamy.
3 Meanwhile, triple-sift flours; sift flour over egg mixture. Pour combined butter and the water down side of bowl then fold ingredients together. Drop rounded tablespoons of mixture into each pan hole.

4 Bake madeleines about 10 minutes. Tap hot pan firmly on bench to release madeleines then turn, top-side down, onto wire rack to cool. Serve dusted with extra sifted icing sugar.

**prep + cook time** 25 minutes **makes** 24 **nutritional count per madeleine** 3.1g total fat (1.9g saturated fat); 222kJ (53 cal); 5.4g carbohydrate; 0.9g protein; 0.1g fibre

# strawberry macaroons

- 3 egg whites
- ¼ cup (55g) caster (superfine) sugar
- pink food colouring
- 2 large (70g) fresh or frozen strawberries
- 1¼ cups (200g) icing (confectioners') sugar
- 1 cup (120g) ground almonds
- ⅓ cup (110g) strawberry jam (conserve)
- 1 tablespoon icing (confectioners') sugar, extra

1 Preheat oven to 150°C/300°F. Grease oven trays; line with baking paper.

2 Beat egg whites in a small bowl with an electric mixer until soft peaks form. Add caster sugar and a few drops colouring, beat until sugar dissolves; transfer mixture to a large bowl.

3 Meanwhile, push strawberries through a fine sieve; you need 1 tablespoon of strawberry puree.

4 Fold sifted icing sugar, ground almonds and strawberry puree into egg white mixture, in two batches.

5 Spoon mixture into a piping bag fitted with a 1cm (½-inch) plain tube. Pipe 4cm (1½-inch) rounds about 2.5cm (1 inch) apart onto trays. Tap trays on bench so macaroons spread slightly. Stand 30 minutes.

6 Bake macaroons about 20 minutes. Cool on trays.

7 Sandwich macaroons with jam. Dust with extra sifted icing sugar.

**prep + cook time**
40 minutes (+ standing)
**makes** 16
**nutritional count per**
**macaroon** 4.1g total fat
(0.3g saturated fat);
489kJ (117 cal);
21.6g carbohydrate;
2.3g protein; 0.8g fibre

**tips** Traditional clafoutis from the Limousin region in central France is made with unpitted cherries. This batter works with many fruits, such as stone fruit, apples or berries.

# plum clafoutis

- 10 small plums (750g), halved, seeded
- ¼ cup (60ml) water
- 1 cinnamon stick, halved
- ¼ cup (55g) firmly packed light brown sugar
- ⅔ cup (160ml) milk
- ⅔ cup (160ml) pouring cream
- 1 teaspoon vanilla extract
- 4 eggs
- ½ cup (110g) caster (superfine) sugar
- ¼ cup (35g) plain (all-purpose) flour

**prep + cook time** 1 hour (+ cooling) **serves** 8 **nutritional count per serving** 22.3g total fat (13.3g saturated fat); 1526kJ (365 cal); 33.8g carbohydrate; 7.5g protein; 0g fibre

1 Preheat oven to 200°C/400°F. Grease a shallow 2.5-litre (10-cup) ovenproof dish.

2 Place plums in a medium baking dish with the water and cinnamon; sprinkle with brown sugar. Cook, in oven, about 15 minutes or until plums soften.

3 Remove cinnamon from dish and place in a medium saucepan with milk, cream and extract; bring to the boil. Cool; remove cinnamon stick.

4 Whisk eggs and caster sugar in a medium bowl until light and frothy; whisk in flour then whisk mixture into cream mixture.

5 Place drained plums in a shallow ovenproof dish; pour cream mixture over plums.

6 Bake clafoutis about 30 minutes or until golden. Serve dusted with icing sugar.

# crêpes suzette

- ¾ cup (110g) plain (all-purpose) flour
- 3 eggs
- 2 tablespoons vegetable oil
- ¾ cup (180ml) milk

### orange sauce

- 125g (4 ounces) unsalted butter
- ½ cup (110g) caster (superfine) sugar
- 1½ cups (375ml) orange juice
- 2 tablespoons lemon juice
- ⅓ cup (80ml) orange-flavoured liqueur

1 Sift flour into a medium bowl, make well in centre; add eggs and oil then gradually whisk in milk until smooth. Pour batter into a large jug. Cover; stand 1 hour.

2 Heat a greased heavy-based crêpe pan or a small frying pan; pour ¼ cup of batter into pan, tilting pan to coat base. Cook, over low heat, until browned, loosening edge of crêpe with spatula. Turn crêpe; brown other side. Remove crêpe from pan; cover to keep warm. Repeat with remaining batter to make a total of eight crêpes, greasing pan each time.

3 Make orange sauce.

4 Fold crêpes in half then in half again, place in sauce; warm over low heat. Remove crêpes and place on serving plates; pour hot sauce over crêpes. Serve with orange segments, if you like.

orange sauce Melt butter in a large frying pan, add sugar; cook, stirring, until mixture begins to brown. Add strained juices; bring to the boil. Reduce heat; simmer, uncovered, about 3 minutes or until a golden colour. Remove from heat; add liqueur, ignite.

**tips** Be very careful when igniting the sauce – use extra long matches, available from most supermarkets or camping stores. Lighting the sauce burns off the alcohol, leaving a more intense flavour. If you prefer, the sauce can be served as is. Make sure overhead exhaust fans are turned off before igniting the sauce.

**prep + cook time** 1 hour
40 minutes (+ standing)
**serves** 4 **nutritional count
per serving** 41g total fat
(20.5g saturated fat); 3039kJ
(727 cal); 66.9g carbohydrate;
10.3g protein; 1.3g fibre

# classic mayonnaise

Whisk 2 egg yolks, ½ teaspoon salt and
1 teaspoon dijon mustard in medium bowl.
Gradually add ⅔ cup extra light olive oil
and ⅓ cup olive oil in a thin, steady stream,
whisking constantly until mixture thickens.
Stir in 1 tablespoon white wine vinegar and
1 tablespoon lemon juice.
**serving suggestion** This sauce goes well
with meats and vegetables, as a sandwich
filling, salad dressing or dipping sauce.

# beurre blanc

Bring ¼ cup dry white wine and
1 tablespoon lemon juice to the boil in
small saucepan. Boil, without stirring, until
reduced by two-thirds. Add ¼ cup pouring
cream; return to the boil then reduce heat.
Whisk in 125g (4 ounces) coarsely chopped
cold butter, piece by piece, whisking
between additions, until sauce is smooth
and has thickened slightly.
**serving suggestion** This sauce goes
well with steamed or grilled salmon and
steamed vegetables.

**prep time** 15 minutes **makes** 1 cup
**nutritional count per tablespoon** 19.2g total fat
(2.9g saturated fat); 719kJ (172 cal);
0g carbohydrate; 0.5g protein; 0g fibre

**prep + cook time** 20 minutes **makes** 1 cup
**nutritional count per tablespoon** 10.4g total fat
(6.8g saturated fat); 406kJ (97 cal);
0.3g carbohydrate; 0.2g protein; 0g fibre

## bordelaise

Combine 2 coarsely chopped shallots (50g), ½ teaspoon crushed dried green peppercorns and 2 cups (500ml) dry red wine in medium saucepan; bring to the boil then reduce heat. Simmer, uncovered, about 15 minutes or until reduced by a third. Add 1½ cups (375ml) beef stock, 1 sprig fresh thyme, 2 dried bay leaves and 2 stalks fresh flat-leaf parsley; bring to the boil then reduce heat. Simmer, uncovered, about 1 hour or until sauce is reduced to ½ cup. Strain, discard herbs. Return sauce to same cleaned pan; stir in 60g (2 ounces) cold unsalted chopped butter, piece by piece, over low heat, until sauce is smooth.

**prep + cook time** 1 hour 35 minutes
**makes** ½ cup **nutritional count per tablespoon** 8.3g total fat (5.5g saturated fat); 568kJ (136 cal); 0.7g carbohydrate; 1.1g protein; 0.1g fibre

## french dressing

Whisk ⅓ cup white wine vinegar and 2 teaspoons dijon mustard in small jug until smooth. Gradually whisk in ⅔ cup olive oil, in a thin steady stream, until thickened.
**serving suggestion** This dressing goes well with any type of salad or salad greens.

**prep time** 5 minutes  **makes** 1 cup
**nutritional count per tablespoon** 12.1g total fat (1.7g saturated fat); 456kJ (109 cal); 0g carbohydrate; 0g protein; 0g fibre

**ALMONDS**

**ground** also called almond meal.

**BACON SLICES** also called bacon rashers.

**BAGUETTE** A French icon, this bread has a crisp golden crust and white, soft filling. It is recognisable by its elongated shape and weighs about 250g. It is the type of bread eaten most in France: either halved with butter for breakfast, with a main meal at lunch or dinner, as a sandwich, or after school with some chocolate.

**BAKING PAPER** also called parchment paper or baking parchment; a silicone-coated paper used to line baking pans and oven trays.

**BAY LEAVES** aromatic leaves from the bay tree available fresh or dried; adds a strong, slightly peppery flavour.

**BEANS**

**green** also called french or string beans; long thin fresh bean is consumed in its entirety once cooked.

**white** a generic term we use for canned or dried cannellini, haricot, navy or great northern beans.

**BEETROOT (BEETS)** firm, round root vegetable.

**BICARBONATE OF SODA** also called baking soda.

**BREADCRUMBS**

**fresh** bread, usually white, processed into crumbs.

**packaged** prepared fine-textured but crunchy white breadcrumbs, good for coating food to be fried.

**BUTTER** we use salted butter unless stated.

**CAPERBERRIES** olive-sized fruit, formed after buds of the caper bush have flowered; usually sold pickled in vinegar brine with stalks intact.

**CAPERS** grey-green buds of a warm climate shrub, sold dried and salted or pickled in a vinegar brine.

**CAPSICUM (BELL PEPPER)** also known as pepper.

**CELERIAC** tuberous root with knobbly brown skin, white flesh and a celery-like flavour. Keep peeled celeriac in acidulated water to stop discolouring. It can be grated and eaten raw in salads; used in soups and stews; boiled and mashed like potatoes; or sliced thinly and deep-fried as chips.

**CHEESE**

**goat's** made from goat's milk; has an earthy, strong taste. Available soft, crumbly and firm, in various shapes and sizes, and sometimes rolled in ash or herbs.

**gruyère** a hard-rind Swiss cheese with small holes and a nutty, slightly salty flavour. A popular cheese for soufflés.

**parmesan** also called parmigiano; a hard, grainy cow's-milk cheese originating in the Parma region of Italy. The curd is salted in brine for a month then aged for up to 2 years.

**roquefort** a blue cheese with a pungent taste; made only from the milk of specially bred sheep. Has a sticky, bone-coloured rind and a creamy, almost shiny interior.

**CHICKEN**

**thigh fillets** thigh with skin and centre bone removed.

**CHOCOLATE**

**dark eating (semi-sweet)** contains a high percentage of cocoa liquor and cocoa butter, and little added sugar. It is ideal for use in desserts and cakes.

**CHORIZO** small, coarse-textured pork and beef Spanish sausages. They are deeply smoked, highly-spiced and dry-cured so that they do not need cooking.

**CINNAMON** available in pieces (sticks or quills) and ground into powder.

**COCOA POWDER** also known as unsweetened cocoa.

**CORNFLOUR** also called cornstarch. Made from corn or wheat.

**CORNICHONS** French for gherkin, a very small type of cucumber. Pickled, they're a traditional accompaniment to pâté, and are also served with a plate of charcuterie (cold meats), fondue or raclette.

**CREAM**

**pouring** also called pure cream. Has no additives, and a minimum fat content of 35 per cent.

**thickened (heavy)** a whipping cream that contains a thickener (minimum fat content of 35 per cent).

**CREME FRAICHE** French for "fresh cream", a fermented cream with a slightly tangy, nutty flavour and velvety texture. Can be used in both sweet and savoury dishes, in much the same way as sour cream. It has the advantage of boiling without curdling.

**DILL** also called dill weed; used fresh or dried, in seed form or ground. Its feathery, frond-like fresh leaves are grassier and more subtle than the dried version or the seeds.

**EGGS** we use large (60g) chicken eggs. If a recipe calls for raw or barely cooked eggs, exercise caution if there is a salmonella problem in your area, particularly in food eaten by children and pregnant women.

**ENDIVE, CURLY** also called frisee, a curly-leafed green vegetable, mainly used in salads.

**FENNEL** also called finocchio or anise; a crunchy green vegetable slightly resembling celery. Dried fennel seeds are also available; they have a stronger licorice flavour.

**FLOUR**

**plain** unbleached wheat flour is the best for baking: the gluten content ensures a strong dough, which produces a light result.

**self-raising** plain or wholemeal flour with baking powder and salt added; make at home in the proportion of 1 cup flour to 2 teaspoons baking powder.

**HONEY** honey sold in a squeezable container is not suitable for the recipes in this book.

**JUNIPER BERRIES** dried berries of an evergreen tree; the main flavouring ingredient in gin.

**KUMARA** the Polynesian name of an orange-fleshed sweet potato often confused with yam; good baked, boiled, mashed or fried similarly to other potatoes.

**LAMB**

**shoulder** large, tasty piece with a lot of connective tissue so is best pot-roasted or braised. Makes the best mince.

**LENTILS, GREEN** or lentils du puy, green-blue (nearly black), tiny lentils with a nutty, earthy flavour and a hardy nature that allows them to be rapidly cooked without disintegrating. French-style green lentils, grown in Victoria, are a local cousin to the expensive French import.

**MAYONNAISE** we use whole-egg mayonnaise; a commercial product of high quality, made with whole eggs and labelled as such.

**MILK** we use full-cream homogenised milk unless stated otherwise.

**MUSHROOMS**

**button** small, cultivated white mushrooms with a mild flavour. When a recipe in this book calls for an unspecified mushroom, use button.

**MUSTARD**

**dijon** Also called french mustard. Pale brown, creamy, fairly mild french mustard. An essential ingredient in French dressings and sauces.

**wholegrain** also called seeded. A French-style coarse-grain mustard made from crushed mustard seeds and dijon-style french mustard.

**NUTMEG** a strong and pungent spice ground from the dried nut of a native Indonesian tree. Usually found ground, the flavour is more intense from a whole nut, available from spice shops, so it's best to grate your own.

**OIL**

**olive** made from ripened olives. Extra virgin and virgin are the first and second press, respectively, and are considered the best; the "extra light" or "light" on other types refers to taste not fat levels.

**vegetable** any number of oils from plant rather than animal fats.

**ONION**

**red** also called spanish, red spanish or bermuda onion; a sweet-flavoured, large, purple-red onion.

**spring** crisp, narrow green-leafed tops and a round sweet white bulb larger than green onions.

**POTATO**

**kipfler (fingerling)** small, finger-shaped, nutty flavour; great baked and in salads.

**ruby lou** oval, with dark pink skin and shallow eyes; has a white flesh and is good for roasting and salads.

**ROCKET (ARUGULA)** also called rucola; peppery green leaf eaten raw or used in cooking. Baby rocket leaves are smaller and less peppery.

**SAFFRON** stigma of a member of the crocus family, available ground or in strands; imparts a yellow-orange colour to food once infused. The quality can vary greatly; the best is the most expensive spice in the world.

**SEAFOOD**

**mussels** should only be bought from a reliable fish market: they must be tightly closed when bought, indicating they are alive. Before cooking, scrub shells with a strong brush to remove beards.

**prawns (shrimp)** can be bought uncooked (green) or cooked, with or without shells.

**scallops** a type of bivalve; often eaten raw or barely seared, they should never be cooked more than 30 seconds as they will lose their juicy tenderness and be tough.

**white fish** non-oily fish; includes bream, flathead, whiting, snapper, redfish, dhufish and ling.

**SHALLOTS** Also called french shallots, eschalots or golden shallots, these are small, elongated, brown-skinned members of the onion family that grow in tight clusters similar to garlic. They are used in sauces, added to salads for extra punch, roasted or caramelised and served with steak.

**SILVER BEET (SWISS CHARD)** known, incorrectly, as spinach. Prepared as for spinach.

**SPINACH** also called english spinach and incorrectly, silver beet. Baby spinach leaves are best eaten raw in salads; the larger leaves should be added last to soups, stews and stir-fries, and should be cooked until barely wilted.

**SUGAR**

**brown** a soft, finely granulated sugar retaining molasses for colour and flavour.

**caster** also called superfine or finely granulated table sugar.

**icing (confectioners')** also called powdered sugar; pulverised granulated sugar crushed together with a small amount of cornflour.

**pure icing (confectioners')** also called powdered sugar.

**raw** natural brown granulated sugar.

**TOMATO**

**canned** whole peeled tomatoes in natural juices; available crushed, chopped or diced. Use undrained.

**paste** triple-concentrated puree used to flavour soups, stews, sauces and casseroles.

**TURMERIC** also called kamin; is a rhizome related to galangal and ginger. Must be grated or pounded to release its acrid aroma and pungent flavour. Known for the golden colour it imparts, fresh turmeric can be substituted with the more commonly found dried powder.

**VANILLA**

**bean** dried, long, thin pod; the minuscule black seeds inside impart a vanilla flavour.

**extract** obtained from vanilla beans infused in water; a non-alcoholic version of essence.

**VINEGAR**

**balsamic** originally from Modena, Italy, there are now many on the market ranging in pungency and quality. Quality can be determined up to a point by price; use the most expensive sparingly.

**cider** made from fermented apples.

**sherry** a natural vinegar made from the sherry grape grown in the southwest of Spain; aged in oak, this traditional wine vinegar has a mellow sweet-sour taste, similar to balsamic vinegar.

**wine** made from red or white wine.

**WATERCRESS** one of the cress family, a large group of peppery greens used raw in salads, dips and sandwiches, or cooked in soups. Highly perishable, so it must be used as soon as possible after purchase.

**WITLOF (BELGIAN ENDIVE)** related to and confused with chicory. A versatile vegetable, it tastes good cooked and raw.

**WORCESTERSHIRE SAUCE** thin, dark-brown spicy sauce; used as a seasoning for meat, gravies and cocktails, and as a condiment.

**ZUCCHINI** also called courgette; harvested when young, its edible flowers can be stuffed and deep-fried.

# conversion chart

## measures

One Australian metric measuring cup holds approximately 250ml, one Australian metric tablespoon holds 20ml, one Australian metric teaspoon holds 5ml. The difference between one country's measuring cups and another's is within a 2- or 3-teaspoon variance, and will not affect your cooking results. North America, New Zealand and the United Kingdom use a 15ml tablespoon. All cup and spoon measurements are level. The most accurate way of measuring dry ingredients is to weigh them. When measuring liquids, use a clear glass or plastic jug with metric markings. We use large eggs with an average weight of 60g.

## dry measures

| METRIC | IMPERIAL |
|--------|----------|
| 15g | ½oz |
| 30g | 1oz |
| 60g | 2oz |
| 90g | 3oz |
| 125g | 4oz (¼lb) |
| 155g | 5oz |
| 185g | 6oz |
| 220g | 7oz |
| 250g | 8oz (½lb) |
| 280g | 9oz |
| 315g | 10oz |
| 345g | 11oz |
| 375g | 12oz (¾lb) |
| 410g | 13oz |
| 440g | 14oz |
| 470g | 15oz |
| 500g | 16oz (1lb) |
| 750g | 24oz (1½lb) |
| 1kg | 32oz (2lb) |

## liquid measures

| METRIC | IMPERIAL |
|--------|----------|
| 30ml | 1 fluid oz |
| 60ml | 2 fluid oz |
| 100ml | 3 fluid oz |
| 125ml | 4 fluid oz |
| 150ml | 5 fluid oz |
| 190ml | 6 fluid oz |
| 250ml | 8 fluid oz |
| 300ml | 10 fluid oz |
| 500ml | 16 fluid oz |
| 600ml | 20 fluid oz |
| 1000ml (1 litre) | 1¾ pints |

## length measures

| METRIC | IMPERIAL |
|--------|----------|
| 3mm | ⅛in |
| 6mm | ¼in |
| 1cm | ½in |
| 2cm | ¾in |
| 2.5cm | 1in |
| 5cm | 2in |
| 6cm | 2½in |
| 8cm | 3in |
| 10cm | 4in |
| 13cm | 5in |
| 15cm | 6in |
| 18cm | 7in |
| 20cm | 8in |
| 23cm | 9in |
| 25cm | 10in |
| 28cm | 11in |
| 30cm | 12in (1ft) |

## oven temperatures

These oven temperatures are only a guide for conventional ovens. For fan-forced ovens, check the manufacturer's manual.

|  | °C (CELSIUS) | °F (FAHRENHEIT) |
|--|--------------|-----------------|
| Very slow | 120 | 250 |
| Slow | 150 | 275-300 |
| Moderately slow | 160 | 325 |
| Moderate | 180 | 350-375 |
| Moderately hot | 200 | 400 |
| Hot | 220 | 425-450 |
| Very hot | 240 | 475 |

The imperial measurements used in these recipes are approximate only. Measurements for cake pans are approximate only. Using same-shaped cake pans of a similar size should not affect the outcome of your baking. We measure the inside top of the cake pan to determine sizes.

# index

Published in 2013 by ACP Books, Sydney

ACP Books are published by ACP Magazines Limited,
a division of Nine Entertainment Co.

54 Park St, Sydney
GPO Box 4088, Sydney, NSW 2001.

phone (+61)2 9282 8618; fax (+61)2 9126 3702

acpbooks@acpmagazines.com.au; www.acpbooks.com.au

ACP Books

Publishing director, ACP Magazines – Gerry Reynolds

Publisher – Sally Wright

Editorial & food director – Pamela Clark

Creative director – Hieu Chi Nguyen

Sales & rights director – Brian Cearnes

Published and Distributed in the United Kingdom by Octopus Publishing Group

Endeavour House

189 Shaftesbury Avenue

London WC2H 8JY

United Kingdom

phone (+44)(0)207 632 5400; fax (+44)(0)207 632 5405

info@octopus-publishing.co.uk;

www.octopusbooks.co.uk

Printed by Toppan Printing Co, China

International foreign language rights - Brian Cearnes, ACP Books  bcearnes@acpmagazines.com.au

A catalogue record for this book is available from the British Library.
ISBN  978-1-74245-236-4